Can AI Craft Communication?

From Richard Tigges

Richard Tigges

Can AI Craft Communication?

Guide to the introduction of
Generative Artificial Intelligence
in PR & Marketing

www.toptext.info

Bibliographic information of the German National Library: The German National Library lists this publication in the German National Bibliography; detailed bibliographic data can be found on the Internet at http://dnb.dnb.de.

Tigges, Richard: Can AI Craft Communication?
Guide to the introduction of Generative Artificial Intelligence in PR & Marketing

© 2025 TOPTEXT Richard Tigges
1st edition

Publisher:
BoD · Books on Demand GmbH, In de Tarpen 42, 22848 Norderstedt, bod@bod.de
Print:
Libri Plureos GmbH, Friedensallee 273, 22763 Hamburg

For the sake of our environment, this book is printed on FSC®-certified paper, which comes from responsible forestry.

ISBN: 978-3-7693-2741-0

Content

Foreword

Artificial intelligence is the technology that deals with the automation of intelligent behavior. The origins of the technology date back to the 20th century, and the disruptive changes to our familiar working world have been questioned on a daily basis since the publication of Chat-GPT at the end of 2022.

In 2017, Google laid the foundation for the GPT [Generative Pretrained Transformer] models with the concept Attention is All You Need.

Since 2023, multimodal models, algorithms that process different data such as text, images and audio simultaneously, have been redefining human-machine interaction. Disruptive technology developments and multi-agent systems are revolutionizing our communication.

With this book "Can AI Craft Communication?", Richard Tigges asks one of the most important questions for the future of our interaction. As an experienced sparring partner and co-lead in the Technology Cluster of the Germany-wide CommTech Association, he knows the needs of his trade.

He combines the skills of journalism, PR and smart technologies in his person and passes them on to PR and marketing departments in this guide. At Volkswagen, in the automotive industry and beyond, he will leave his mark with his commitment to data- and AI-driven communication. I appreciate his visionary power

Have fun reading and learning!

Daniela Rittmeier
Head of [Generative] AI Accelerator, Capgemini

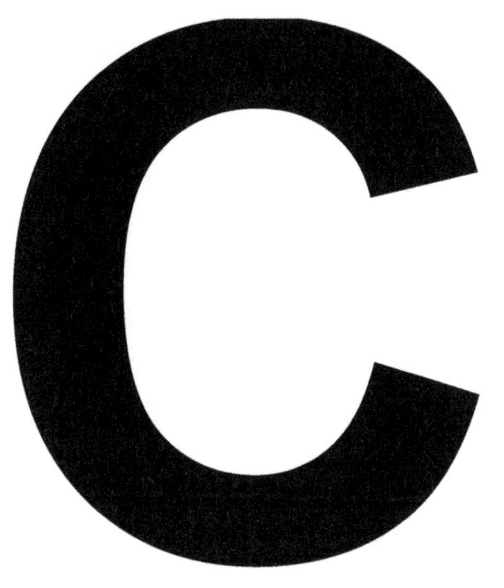

an AI Craft Communication? And how do I put our company at the forefront of the Generative AI [GenAI] movement or at least among the fast followers? There are actually far more communication professionals dealing with this question at the moment than would like to admit. In this guide, I will take away some of the fear of taking the first (or second) step and give you concrete suggestions in the following chapter on how to introduce AI in your PR or marketing department quickly, efficiently and, above all, in a meaningful way. There are quick wins and long-term, strategic decisions that will pay off.

The new generation of communicators is no longer streaming into professional life as "GenZ" from universities, but from the AI labs of this world. They call themselves "GenAI" and promise to master the basics of PR & marketing. And to fulfill large parts of the job description of "communications expert" straight away. Almost without training. This is the expertise of the groundbreaking technology that we call Generative Artificial Intelligence (GenAI for short).

As flesh-and-blood communicators, we are right on the cusp of using GenAI on a large scale and want everyone to benefit from it as early, as comprehensively and as error-free as possible. At the same time, there is no time to lose. As chance would have it, this huge upheaval is taking place in the midst of global wars and crises and as well in post-pandemic times. In a tense economic situation, a number of companies are under great pressure to be efficient. Technology that promises to produce content for communication in the blink of an eye, automate processes and individualize the way target groups are addressed like never before comes in handy. In the public debate, cost-cutting measures or even redundancies are increasingly being mentioned in the same breath as AI, which has given GenAI the involuntary image of a job killer. It is not only an amplifier of creativity for our profession, but also an amplifier of efficiency.

After **OpenAI** presented its generative pre-trained transformers under the name GPT in November 2022, the first product called **ChatGPT** caused a worldwide sensation. Within a few days, more than 100 million users were already using the program – the fastest growing platform of all time had been launched. Since then, generative artificial intelligence has reached all areas of life and work and has had a disruptive effect like nothing before.

ChatGPT was not the end of the story. OpenAI added more powerful versions of its text-to-image generator **DALL-E** from year to year and presented an initial preview of the **Sora** text-to-video generator in February 2024, which was launched in December of the same year. In addition to text, images and moving images, voices and music can also be generated in impressive quality.

Missing a month of AI feels like missing a year. This is because the new technology of generative AI challenges us to keep pace every day. Regardless of whether OpenAI's GPT, Llama, Claude, Gemini or DeepSeek from China is the better language model, GenAI will only provide us communicators with active support if it is seamlessly integrated into our daily work.

To implement generative artificial intelligence and data-based recommendations for action in PR & marketing, I recommend a clear strategy with a roadmap that outlines the gradual integration of AI along the value chain.

- Message library and AI message tracking
- Prompt library with format descriptions
- Efficient AI content workflows
- Journalist service with chatbot
- Hyperpersonalization in PR & Marketing
- Automated reporting
- Automated asset production
- Real-time performance and sentiment analyses
- Outside-in impulses
- AI optimization of content
- Customized individual training

In the following, I will describe in more detail what I consider to be the twelve most important application areas with which you should ideally start building your AI workshop.

Write down messages and work with semantic vectors

Modern communication demands precision and consistency. It is therefore important to first define WHAT a company has to say. Surprisingly, very few PR and marketing departments have a proper message management system in which the central content is available in writing, accessible to the entire team and always up to date. This includes figures, data and facts as well as the collection of active statements about the company and its products or services and reactive statements for known crisis topics or holding statements for potential further crises

Such a one-voice library is not rocket science. It simply requires the discipline to first complete the common homework implementing specific content in the individual silos of a communications department:

- Researching a topic
- Identification of unique selling points
- Strategic evaluation of the topic
- Focusing on central statements/messages
- Anticipation of possible counterarguments in a Q&A

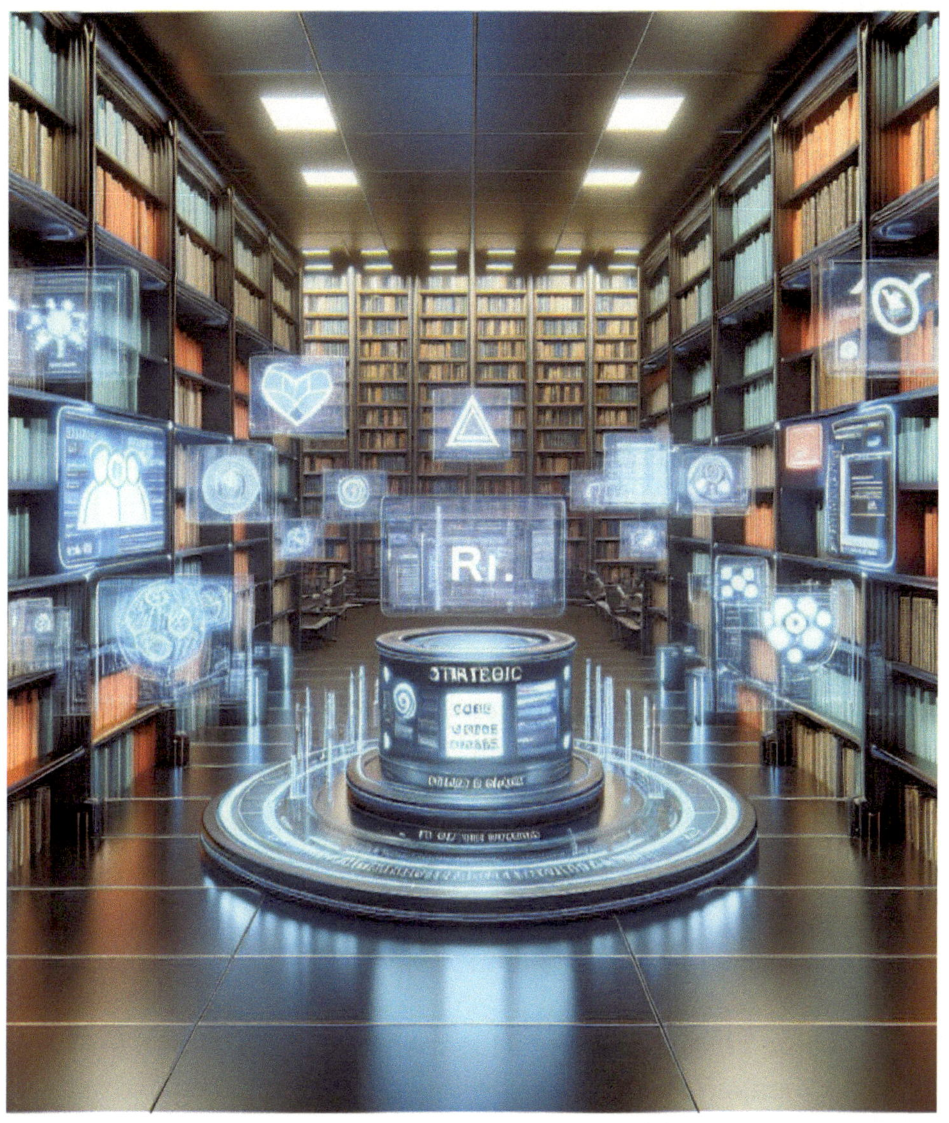

Since GenAI began to take effect, more and more communications departments are recognizing the importance of strategic message management. After all, the output can only be as good as the input. I like to call messages as a source of structured input the "Maggi cube of communication", because they can later be used to prepare a wide variety of dishes for a wide variety of occasions and tastes.

At this point, gourmets usually turn up their noses at my banal comparison. But when I remind them that they also stroll through the market to enjoy a good meal with friends, select the best ingredients, bring them fresh to the table and often conjure up something fantastic from some of the ingredients the following day, then they understand the comparison. And if you plan to serve thousands of dishes a year, you need to start paying attention to the consistent quality of the ingredients. In any case, it's worth putting time and love into the essence of communication.

Message management is the ideal frontloading for communication, not just with regard to AI. That's why building a one-voice library should have been the first step in digitizing your communications department; do it now at the latest. In my opinion, **YessPress®** has integrated the best tool for message management into its **ComTool** and linked it to GenAI. The Erlangen-based company has developed another AI solution for digitizing an initial stock of statements and Q&As, which condenses archived speeches, press releases, etc. into core statements and Q&As based on the most common journalistic criteria.

At the same time, the use of AI in media analysis allows the most exciting measurement since the invention of the "Pressespiegel" for the first time. At last, it is no longer just about the height of the clipping stack in centimetres, the advertising equivalent in euros, the number of articles published or their cumulative reach or the admittedly superficial assessment of the overall article as "positive", "neutral" or "negative". Finally, the first providers such as **Altastic** can measure exactly what should be in the best interest of every PR department: How do we get through to the media with our key messages?

Such an analysis is possible with the help of semantic vectorization. In this process, statements are localized according to their meaning in the multidimensional meaning space. In-house messages undergo vectorization, as do full-text media references. By comparing the vectors, the global response to messages can be continuously tracked – regardless of formulation and language. Audi, Altastic and YessPress were the first to set up this use case in 2024 and are evaluating up to 400,000 references every day. AI message tracking is an invaluable tool for taking strategic communication to a new level.

But even if you are not currently planning AI-based media monitoring in your company, I strongly recommend that you at least set up a message library. This decision will change the way you communicate! For the implementation of a global OneVoice policy. And for a low-effort "feeding" of all GenAI applications that you plan to use in the future.

Prompt library instead of live user prompts

If you want to communicate strategically – especially in times of GenAI – you cannot avoid a detailed description of your in-house communication formats. If the messages are the WHAT of communication, you define the HOW in the formats.

- How is a press release from our brand structured?
- What does our CEO look for in an internal speech?
- What do we mean by this Twinkle in the Eye at the end of our LinkedIn Longreads
- What does an intranet message look like for us?

If you don't want to think about this every time you use GenAI, you can call up the predefined format descriptions instead of entering live user prompts. All you need to do is set up a prompt library (similar to the message library described above). Although the first generic products are available on the market that can be used to generate acceptable results for a variety of communication formats, you will achieve the best results with a specific description of your in-house text types. So make sure that your central communication tool can be expanded to include a prompt library.

To stay with the image of the Maggi cube (or perhaps better the "essence of communication"): Standardizing the best recipes is a prerequisite for scaling AI content production in order to get out of the trial run of the AI witches' kitchen

The car manufacturer **Audi** and **Deutsche Bahn** use their digital message libraries, aptly named OneVoice, and their own prompt library in YessPress® ComTool to largely dispense with live user prompts and corresponding individual training for communicators.

The philosophy behind this is that a company does not spontaneously think about what it has to say with every prompt, nor how its communication formats are structured. The "what" and "how" lie in the message and prompt libraries.

The user compiles the appropriate messages in a shopping cart system and selects the desired format and language style depending on the target group. The user can also send the current hook or important directional instructions to the AI as additional direct instructions.

This process speeds up the work and ensures the quality of the generated texts. The prompt library allows access to the AI expertise of other experts and media companies without them having to explicitly disclose their knowledge. GenAI has thus arrived in the sharing economy.

E fficient workflows with AI support

AI-supported tools make it possible to create a variety of derivatives from central messages and prepared format descriptions, each of which is perfectly tailored to a platform and personalized to the target group.

Efficient content workflows are essential here, from the board of directors' address to the social media post, in order to always involve people where they perform controlling, deciding, correcting or approving functions, despite all the automation of content production.

The daily flood of information makes it difficult for people to identify relevant content themselves. This is where process support from AI comes into play: it transcribes meetings or interviews, summarizes research concisely and identifies key statements. It is aware of trends and alerts us when we need to turn the communication tide. This makes the work of us communicators more effective, as important details are no longer overlooked.

The approach of interwoven workflows between AI and humans saves time and ensures quality. Because despite all our enthusiasm for technology, we have to ensure that the results with GenAI are not just "cool" or "pretty good", but correspond 100 percent to what our companies have to say and how we want to say it.

The key difference to conventional process workflows is that AI workflows do not necessarily have to be initiated by humans. After all, the special power of artificial intelligence is to provide us with answers to questions that we haven't even asked yet. This is what makes GenAI so valuable as an assistant. If an algorithm recognizes that several factors have occurred that make a workflow between man and machine necessary, then it starts it!

Journalist services improve with AI chatbot

Increasing the response speed of press offices is essential for improved media relations. An intelligent chat robot revolutionizes the service for journalists overnight: instead of waiting for callbacks or having to read extensive FAQs, journalists receive quick, precise answers to their questions around the clock on your press website. AI could cluster journalist inquiries received by email according to topic and use them to create a tag cloud in the spirit of predictive communications. In the next step, it would search for answers to the questions. You have a treasure trove of answers if you have followed my first piece of advice and built up a one-voice library. And to make the communication more personal, references to the journalist's previous publications could be inserted automatically. The press department only checks the drafts and concentrates on speaking to the media, pitching stories and further relationship building.

I recommend that the bot (in addition to the usual severability clause that the content is created by AI and there is no 100 percent guarantee of accuracy) always refers to the expert on this topic in the press department and offers to contact the journalist at the next opportunity. This increases the acceptance of such automation on both sides of the desk and places the human component of media relations in the foreground. Nevertheless, a chatbot is a useful addition: it reduces waiting times, increases satisfaction and strengthens the relationship with media representatives.

What works on the website for a single question can also be used for bundles of media inquiries received by phone or email. A duplicate comparison can also be carried out here to get to grips with the practice of some journalists scattering their inquiries across the company every minute and trying out whether the company contradicts itself

In addition, a tag cloud can be created as a by-product of the AI processing of media inquiries, which the head of the communications department can use to recognize what the most media inquiries currently relate to. The result is almost like a predictive media review for the next day.

Hyper-personalization in PR & Marketing

In order to address multipliers and target groups in a targeted manner, communication must be individually tailored to their interests. GenAI makes it possible to precisely analyze these interests. In this way, messages can be used in a targeted manner to attract attention.

In press and public relations work, the path of hyper-personalization with GenAI means conducting a tailored dialogue with our stakeholders. After all, we know that in today's communications landscape, traditional one-way communication based on the "sender to receiver" principle is passé. Hyper-personalization enables PR professionals to interact with journalists not only in a targeted manner, but on an (almost) individual level

The principle is simple: instead of sending out blanket press releases, PR teams use GenAI to analyze the previously expressed interests, publications and even the writing style of the top journalists relevant to this company. Based on this data, the multipliers can be contacted in a personalized manner. They only receive topics that make sense for them and their medium. And they receive a letter that speaks to them personally because it is formulated "in their language". This strengthens trust in the sender.

For example, data analysis could show that a journalist frequently reports on technology and its social impact. The PR department could then develop a story that focuses, for example, on ethical aspects of AI – a topic that is clearly based on the journalist's interests. This approach not only makes the approach more effective, but also more credible, as it respects and responds to the individual profile of the recipient. Such emails or calls are not seen as promotional, but useful.

However, the limits of hyper-personalization lie in its implementation. Overly personalized messages can give journalists an uncomfortable feeling of being "monitored" if they get the impression that their privacy is being violated. PR professionals must therefore find the fine line between data-based precision and ethically sound communication. At the same time, the method offers an opportunity to build deeper relationships with media representatives by highlighting the true value of a message in context.

While PR influences journalists and influencers to encourage them to publish in the media, hyper-personalization in marketing takes individualization to the extreme. Modern technologies make it possible to analyze the customer journey of each individual customer in such detail that marketing strategies can be broken down to "N=1" – this means a tailored approach for each individual customer. This goal of hyper-personalization is tantamount to the individualization of communication.

Tailoring content to different target groups to an extent that no communication department could achieve without technical support is a large part of GenAI's potential for our profession. But in order for GenAI to create hyper-personalized content, it needs knowledge about its customers. This is why strengths such as emotional intelligence, empathy and active listening are particularly in demand in marketing and communication.

The e-commerce sector serves as a model here: instead of general product recommendations, customers already receive suggestions that are precisely tailored to their purchase history, browsing activities and even behavioral patterns. A customer who recently searched for running clothes will not only receive a suitable offer for running shoes, but also a recommendation for training plans or nutrition programs – all tailored to her presumed needs.

The technical basis for further hyper-personalization in marketing is provided by AI algorithms that can recognize and adapt patterns in real time. Even the choice of communication channel is being hyper-personalized: Some customers respond better to e-mails, others prefer social media approaches or personalized ads. The aim is to create communication that is so seamless and relevant that the customer feels optimally understood.

But there are challenges here too: Data protection and ethical boundaries are key issues. Companies that rely on hyper-personalization must communicate transparently how and why data is used in order to retain the trust of their customers. If this succeeds, marketing becomes not just advertising, but real added value – a dialog that starts exactly where the customer is at the moment.

Automation for routine topics

When it comes to stock market reports, local election results and regional sporting events, we have already become accustomed to reports that are written by algorithms rather than journalists.

Depending on the data, the AI finds suitable phrases such as "leap forward", "neck-and-neck race" or "last-minute home win". The advantage of automated reporting on these winner-loser topics is that large amounts of data can be broken down into very small units of information, each of which is only of interest to a small group of readers, and these can be automatically processed into continuous text.

Automated reporting will become an indispensable part of modern PR work in addition to entering the media "on the other side of the desk". To realize this, you first need to create a solid data infrastructure. This includes linking internal and external data sources – such as real-time sensor technology, social media analyses or operational information. The better your company's data domains are organized, the easier it is to automate reports from production, sales, finance, etc. The collected data must be brought together in a central system that processes and interprets it automatically and converts it into text.

Many companies are currently rethinking their data domains, a kind of reversal of the burden of proof, as a lawyer would say. In the past, someone who needed the data of another department had to justify this in detail. Today, it's the norm for all data to be available. The department holding the data would have to justify why it wants to deviate from this. If data really is the treasure of the 21st century, as is so often claimed, then this treasure belongs to the company and not to individual departments!

A practical example from the public sector: in the event of a train breakdown, AI systems could analyze data from rail operations, passenger information and weather forecasts to create a precise message in a matter of seconds. This message could be sent directly to various channels, from social media to individual push notifications, in a language adapted to the target group. Automation makes communication not only fast and consistent, but also personalized.

A further step for the introduction of such automated reporting is the development of a "content kit". After all, you probably don't want to leave it entirely up to GenAI to decide how an automated report is structured. It is therefore advisable to use ready-made text modules that can be flexibly combined with real-time data. In this way, even complex situations can be communicated efficiently and clearly

Finally, it is crucial not to neglect the human factor. Automated systems should be designed in such a way, , that they can be monitored by PR teams and adjusted if necessary. Especially in sensitive crisis situations, it is important that automation adheres to ethical standards and does not spread misleading or inappropriate messages. A balance of AI efficiency and human sensitivity guarantees that automated reporting not only works technically, but is also used strategically.

Automated asset production

The rapid pace that social media imposes on us requires companies to produce content in a constant and targeted manner. Artificial intelligence (AI) plays a crucial role in this by enabling the automated creation of assets such as images, videos or audio clips. This technological advancement not only increases the efficiency of content production, but also increases the ability to react to current trends in real time during ongoing campaigns. The ability of AI to adapt content to current developments in real time is particularly valuable. By analyzing user behavior and current topics, AI can dynamically shape content to achieve maximum relevance and engagement. This leads to increased responsiveness and enables target groups to be addressed more effectively.

In the asset management of the future, text content is automatically combined with suitable visual and audio media. Photos, videos and audio files are thus precisely coordinated with the text messages, creating a coherent and appealing user experience.

The two major providers of AI video avatars are **HeyGen** and **Synthesia**. Both offer lifelike avatars inspired by actors. For around 1,000 US dollars a year, you can even create an avatar from your own studio material that has the voice and appearance of its owner. Users can enter text scripts that are presented by realistic-looking avatars in over 60 languages. This makes the production of training and marketing videos much easier and ensures that the desired messages are conveyed consistently. Existing videos can be lip-synced for international versions at the touch of a button.

Online shoe retailer Zalando and online mail order company Otto Group were among the first retailers to present their products to the public with the help of artificial models. New outfits, any background, no stress with highly paid, sometimes unconventional models, no travel costs, no time pressure on set. Initially, the fashion was still worn by human body models during photography and the heads were later replaced by avatars in post-production because the AI did not yet allow clothes and bodies to harmonize perfectly with each other. Spanish fashion label Mango took the next step in 2024 and had a model created entirely by GenAI appear for its youthful Sunset Dream Collection. 72% of customers did not even recognize the fake, according to a survey conducted by market research institute Appinio during the ongoing campaign.

Avatars that speak sign language can be used for barrier-free communication. Six medium-sized partners in Germany carried out the **AVASAG** project from 2020 to 2023 in order to better involve the approximately 70 million deaf people worldwide in digital visual communication.

AI-supported tools such as **Flick** or **JasperAI** make the creation of social media content much easier. Among other things, they allow users to create personalized and brand-appropriate subtitles for their posts, which also significantly reduces the effort involved in content creation.

In the audiovisual sector, **Elevenlabs** offers natural-sounding speech synthesis thanks to deep learning. The platform enables the conversion of text into high-quality, human-like speech in 32 languages, making it ideal for applications such as audio books, video voice recordings and commercials. An outstanding feature of ElevenLabs is its voice creation capability. Users can generate unique voices through text input alone, providing a wide range of voice characteristics for different applications. ElevenLabs also offers the possibility of voice cloning. All you need to do is upload at least 30 minutes of audio material from your own voice as training data and then prove in a live test that it is your own voice. This makes it possible to have entire books converted into audio

books using your own voice or to produce multilingual audio material in languages that you don't even speak yourself. Another

feature of Elevenlabs is sound effects that are created from descriptive text input.

Audiate, on the other hand, enables the editing of audio and video content on a text-based level by converting spoken words into text.

This allows users to edit their recordings efficiently and match the audio content precisely to the texts.

Another tool is **Predis.ai**, a free AI social media post generator. With Predis.ai, users can generate impressive social media posts by making simple inputs and letting the AI do the creative work. This makes it possible to efficiently fill social media channels with high-quality content. However, most users recognize this GenAI content by its typical structure and the fact that it is not a human thought with rough edges, but a polished and ultimately interchangeable text – because it tries to generate output with little input and little effort.

GenAI has the potential to fundamentally transform asset management. By automating the creation and adaptation of photos, videos and audio files that are perfectly matched to the respective text content, companies can create consistent and engaging multimedia experiences.

AI-supported image and video editing tools can automatically adapt photos and videos to specific requirements, for example by changing backgrounds or adding certain visual effects. This enables companies to adapt their visual content flexibly and efficiently to different campaigns or platforms. Not only can they increase efficiency, but they can also tailor content precisely to the needs and interests of target groups. This leads to improved brand perception and strengthens the bond with stakeholders.

Performance and sentiment analyses in real-time

Measuring success in corporate communications has reached a new dimension through the use of artificial intelligence (AI). Media intelligence agencies such as Altastic are at the forefront of this development and demonstrate how AI can bring about transformative changes in media monitoring and analysis. With AI-supported dashboards, key performance indicators (KPIs) such as reach, engagement and tonality are displayed in real time and can therefore be monitored and tracked. Data-based control makes it possible to deploy resources in a targeted manner and continuously optimize success.

Thanks to AI, several hundred thousand cross-media hits from the global media can be analyzed every day. Compared to the previous limitation to a representative media set, the new approach is equivalent to a full survey. Altastic also keeps an eye on television, radio and podcasts and has fully integrated social media into this setup for better comparability.

AI-based media monitoring works with semantic vectorization, i.e. a formulation- and language-independent localization of terms in the meaning space as well as with the automatic recognition of entities such as institutions, objects or people. Brand logos, faces, fonts and tonality are automatically recognized and assigned, audio is transcribed and social media is integrated. All of this allows for refined analyses, including the question of which press photo in which format was used more frequently by the media in order to optimize the next asset production according to demand. In future, the success of a communications department will certainly no longer be measured by the number of press releases sent out or the reach they achieve, but primarily by the degree of message penetration in the media and the associated sentiment.

Sentiment analysis also plays a role in monitoring general channels, known as listening. AI-based sentiment analysis makes it possible to monitor sentiment on social networks and other channels in real time. This enables companies to identify trends at an early stage, prevent potential crises and react to negative developments before they escalate. This is particularly valuable when it comes to understanding public opinion and acting accordingly. The real-time capability of the analyses is crucial here. The ability to process and interpret large amounts of data in real time enables companies to make well-founded, data-based decisions. Communicators can react immediately to changes in public perception, enabling a proactive rather than reactive communication strategy. This leads to a stronger brand perception and increased customer loyalty, as companies are able to respond to the needs and moods of their target groups.

O utside-in impulses matched with your own comms plans

A fundamental change in perspective can be accelerated by artificial intelligence if companies no longer see themselves as broadcasters who spread their messages inside-out, but as participants in a dialog. This forces them to listen better, absorb and organize outside-in impulses and use them as a hook for contributing to the public debate. The more data is analyzed about the communicative environment, the clearer the risks and opportunities become to join in the discussion and put other aspects up for debate.

The use of GenAI is also becoming increasingly important for "agenda surfing". This approach enables companies to identify current public debates and trends and adapt their communication accordingly. By using GenAI, communicators can analyze the public agenda and gain valuable outside-in insights to determine the optimal timing and approach for their messages.

To do this, large amounts of data from various sources such as social media, news portals and forums are analyzed in real time. By identifying key topics and moods within the target group, companies can tailor their communication content precisely to current interests and needs. This increases the likelihood that the messages will resonate and have the desired effect.

A practical example of the use of GenAI in agenda surfing is the use of AI-supported monitoring tools that continuously monitor the media environment in "listening" and identify relevant topics and emerging trends. These tools can help companies to react proactively to changes in public opinion. In addition, GenAI can help to identify potential crises at an early stage by detecting negative sentiment or critical discussions in the media. This enables companies to take countermeasures in good time to avoid reputational damage.

In a pilot project between **Deutsche Presse-Agentur** (dpa) and YessPress®, GenAI was used to automatically compare around 10,000 current events from politics, business and society as well as international anniversaries with planned corporate communication measures. Suitable events that could increase success are immediately identified. The same applies to disruptive press events that would divert media attention

The use of GenAI for outside-in impulses in corporate communications makes it possible to effectively utilize current public debates and trends. The valuable outside-in impulses enable communicators to choose the right time and the right story angle for their content in order to achieve maximum resonance.

Content optimization with GenAI

In digital communication, it is becoming increasingly important to optimize content not only for human readers, but also for artificial intelligence. Similar to the optimization of texts for search engines such as Google or Bing (SEO), Generative Engine Optimization (GEO) aims to structure and present information in such a way that it can be easily recognized, interpreted and further processed by algorithms. This is crucial to ensure that messages are findable and effective in the digital world.

A clear and logical structure of the content is essential here. By using headings, paragraphs and lists (e.g. with advantages and disadvantages of a topic), information can be organized hierarchically and thus made more accessible for AI systems. In addition, metadata such as titles, descriptions and keywords should be carefully selected to emphasize the context and relevance of the content. The use of standardized data formats and semantic markups can also help AI algorithms to better understand, assign and process the content.

The quality of the content also plays a decisive role. AI systems are increasingly able to assess the relevance and authenticity of information. It is therefore important to provide accurate, up-to-date and trustworthy information. The inclusion of references and further links can increase credibility and at the same time add value for the user. Optimizing content for AI not only improves visibility in digital channels, but also increases the effectiveness of communication.

In summary, corporate messages should be findable in the new world of AI assistants. Content can be optimized for AI in a similar way to search engine optimization. Information must be structured as well as possible so that it can be easily recognized, interpreted and processed by algorithms.

But there's more: journalistic writing rules, including the famous theorems of the late journalist Wolf Schneider, search engine optimization rules, company spelling and the style guide or tone of voice of the respective sender should (in the right order, so that the house rules "have the last word") check texts via automated content optimization loops and make correction suggestions (and are happy to do so). GenAi checks everything – machine and manually created texts – to ensure a uniform quality standard.

Media trainings for interviewees with GenAI

Board members, technical experts, press spokespersons – they all benefit from practising media interviews and practising a wide range of situations and skills. How do I react to awkward questions? How do I convey my key messages regardless of the questions? What do I do with provocation and where do I have to make a clear cut? How do I answer in such a way that I come across as competent and likeable at the same time? It is common practice to bring in media trainers who have gained sufficient experience with interviews, interviewers and interviewees as a presenter, reporter or former company spokesperson.

However, time and costs usually stand in the way of regular training sessions. So, it would be really handy to be interviewed by a virtual journalist for practice in between. I recently created an AI interview trainer with the Berlin start-up **cuinti**. The user selects a subject area, a language, a medium and the desired level of difficulty and is then interviewed by telephone. The course of the conversation with this virtual journalist is not planned in advance and depends very much on my answers

As soon as I hang up, the result appears on the screen in the form of a detailed analysis: How strong was I on the relationship level? Did I address the other person by name, did I talk to them personally before the conversation started? Did I respond to the other person? Was I patient enough? Where did I miss an opportunity? Did I get my message across? And how was my speaking style, especially in a foreign language?

It is important that such an analysis is only available for download by the person being trained and is deleted immediately. A detailed report after the simulated interview situation can then be a good basis for the next personal training session. Imparting knowledge is more important than ever in a time of rapid change. This is the only way we communicators can stay up-to-date and constantly expand our skillset. Combining the possibilities of GenAI results in customized individual training courses:

- be addressed by name
- on topics that interest me
- with examples that appeal to me personally

- with avatars that I have chosen or that embody people from my professional environment
- in a language in which I would like to train at the moment
- faster when I am strong, slower when I am weak
- Completely flexible in terms of time, can be interrupted at any time

Communicators benefit from customized training courses that are developed with the help of AI. The AI adapts to the individual strengths and weaknesses of the participants and offers a personalized learning experience that has a lasting effect.

Transformation brings up training needs within the team

While we have already talked about the benefits for the training and further education of communicators in general in the previous section, we should not forget one thing: GenAI came, saw and conquered. To ensure that our teams don't feel lost and that we make sure that they use the new technology in the best interests of the company (including the IT, information security, legal and works council departments), GenAI should be on the timetable!
General knowledge about the opportunities and risks of artificial intelligence and ethical issues are just as much a part of this as the specific use in your PR or marketing department. Which tools do we use and how, how do we label AI-generated contributions and what else needs to be considered? As GenAI is a young field of technology, the training courses need to be updated on an ongoing basis.

People without in-depth programming knowledge often believe that they lack this as a key qualification for a professional use of GenAI that goes into depth. The most important skill – and this applies to all industries – that even an advanced user of generative AI should have is their own specialist expertise, in our case a deep understanding of press relations or marketing. This reassuring realization has already astonished many visitors to presentations and workshops.

Take the team's fears seriously and discuss them together. The introduction of AI must not be a secret project. Success simply lies in the participation of those affected in shaping their future. A number of differently motivated concerns about GenAI are to be expected. What these are and how they are dealt with is the subject of the second chapter. The best way to deal with resistance is to make a serious attempt to understand the motivation behind it. The triggers for fears that are usually very easy to understand range from your own economic existence to your own understanding of your profession and general questions. I will deal with the following in more detail:

- Loss of jobs
- Loss of quality in communication
- Lack of control over the communication process
- Data protection concerns
- Resistance to change

It should also be noted that the fears expressed do not always correspond to the fears felt. This discrepancy can be attributed to various psychological mechanisms.

A central aspect is **self-presentation**: people tend to conceal or modify their true feelings in order to meet the expectations of their social environment or to convey a certain image of themselves. This behavior can lead to a situation where the fears expressed do not match the fears actually felt. **Social desirability** and **stigmatization of opponents** can lead to individuals not openly communicating certain fears for fear of negative evaluation or rejection. This increases the discrepancy between expressed and perceived fears. If consent to AI is socially desirable, team members may play along on the surface. In order to really find out what moves them, there needs to be room for openness.

Another relevant mechanism is **cognitive dissonance**. When individuals have thoughts or feelings that contradict their self-image or beliefs, this can cause discomfort. To reduce this discomfort, they may adjust their expressed fears so that they are more in line with their self-image or social norms.

Emotional awareness also plays a role. Some people are not fully aware of their own fears or have difficulty identifying and expressing them clearly. This can lead to the expressed fears not reflecting the actual inner feelings. GenAI is a new topic that many people only know from science fiction novels. Suddenly, "colleague computer" is really on the scene.

Understanding these mechanisms is crucial in order to grasp the complexity of human emotions and expressions and to be able to react appropriately.

Job loss as an existential fear coming up with the power of AI

The integration of artificial intelligence (AI) in companies is currently giving rise to justified fears in many companies regarding the loss of jobs. Employees are worried that automated systems will take over their tasks, making them redundant. These fears are understandable, but it is important to emphasize that in many cases AI serves as a supporting tool that takes over repetitive and monotonous tasks. This gives employees more room for strategic, creative and complex activities that require human judgment and empathy.

One example of this is the use of AI in customer service. Automated chatbots can answer frequently asked questions and solve simple problems, freeing up human employees. They can then concentrate on more demanding customer concerns in second-level support that require personalized solutions. This division of labor not only increases efficiency, but also increases employee job satisfaction as they can focus on challenging and fulfilling tasks.

The use of AI also opens up new professional fields and areas of activity. There is a need for specialists who develop, implement and monitor AI systems. There is also a need for experts who can optimize collaboration between humans and machines and take ethical and legal aspects into account. Employees can expand their skills and qualify for these new roles through appropriate further training measures.

Which typical characteristics remain in demand in PR & marketing because no AI can replace them? For a long time, we consoled ourselves with the idea that AI only reproduces something that already exists and does not create anything new. But GenAI can no longer be denied a certain kind of creativity. Should that scare us? Should we fear GenAI as a job killer? The short answer could even be a provocative one: Yes!

And here is the more detailed one: Anyone who believes that GenAI is a temporary phenomenon that we can ignore is mistaken. Those who do not engage with the technology and the new possibilities will lack the skills they need to succeed in the future. This is comparable to innovations such as the typewriter, the telephone and the Internet. It is unthinkable that we would still be keeping up to date with handwritten letters today.

In addition to generating media content, GenAI can also support and take on far more complex approaches than just the much-cited "repetitive tasks". This raises the question of whether GenAI complements or substitutes the classic personality type of corporate communication. If one assumes that communication professionals are on average more creative, artistic and communicative, then structural thinking, analysis, thoroughness and repetition to perfection tend to be less pronounced cliché attributions for this job profile. This clearly suggests that GenAI can complement communicators very well and not necessarily replace them. At least for the time being.

The question of whether GenAI could make communicators superfluous because other departments have acquired new communication skills overnight can also be answered in the negative – for the time being. Anyone who is aware of the governance of a company's communication should be pleased to experience a new quality of collaboration, namely when AI "thinks things through" and prepares better briefings for the specialist departments in future. Perhaps there will soon be GPT templates for non-communicators so that AI can conduct dialog-based research with them?

Of course, job profiles will change massively. The traditional speechwriter may become a message manager. The traditional illustrator may become an AIAD expert. The traditional author may become a final editor. And ideally, we will encounter the skills shortage with AI solutions. AI is supposed to save money and time, improve quality and increase independence (from consultants or agencies). At the same time, we must bear in mind that GenAI has triggered an arms race between media and communications departments. Business journalists and analysts are making heavy use of AI to get to the bottom of business information. This will inevitably lead to companies having to expand their financial and crisis communications.

In other words, nobody needs to be afraid of GenAI as a job killer. The technology will trigger the most massive transformation of communication work ever. Used correctly, it is a powerful tool. It is therefore crucial to have open communication about the introduction of AI in the company. Employees should be involved in the change process and informed about the benefits and opportunities. Transparency and training can strengthen trust in the technology and promote acceptance. In this way, AI is not perceived as a threat, but as an opportunity for personal and professional growth.

Quality loss as a counterargument to GenAI

As a new colleague, AI will be watched with suspicious eyes and its mistakes will be judged particularly critically. Quick wins that demonstrate how AI can generate high-quality and targeted content are important here.

The introduction of AI into corporate communications is often viewed with skepticism, particularly with regard to the quality of the content generated. There is concern that automated texts or responses will not achieve the same level of precision and creativity as human contributions. To address these concerns, it is important to highlight the capabilities of modern AI systems and demonstrate their potential through concrete examples.

AI-supported tools can help to analyze large amounts of data and derive relevant information for communication. They are able to create personalized content that is tailored to the needs and interests of the target group. The automation of routine tasks also increases efficiency so that human employees have more time for creative and strategic activities.

To ensure the quality of AI-generated content, it is important to define clear guidelines and standards. Human monitoring and regular quality checks are essential to ensure that the messages correspond to the company's values and are correct. By combining AI and human expertise, high quality communication can be guaranteed.

Another aspect is the continuous improvement of AI systems through feedback and learning. The more data and feedback the AI receives, the better it can adapt and optimize its performance. Companies should therefore implement mechanisms that allow experience and findings to be incorporated into the further development of AI.

Lack of control over the communication process

The introduction of AI into communication processes can cause employees to fear losing control over important processes. The fear arises that automated systems will make decisions independently, without human intervention or monitoring.

In practice, this means that AI systems can take over tasks such as data analysis, pattern recognition or the creation of drafts, while the final decision and fine-tuning remain in human hands. This division of labor makes it possible to increase efficiency without losing control of the communication process. Human expertise remains essential to bring context, nuances and ethical considerations to the communication.

To increase trust in AI-supported processes, companies should establish transparent workflows that clearly define which tasks are performed by AI and which by humans. Regular training and workshops can help to deepen understanding of how AI works and provide employees with the skills they need to interact effectively with the technology.

It is also important to set up feedback loops that make it possible to continuously monitor the performance of the AI and make adjustments if necessary. These measures ensure that the AI acts as an extension of the human communicator and that the desired messages are conveyed accurately and effectively.

Before each phase of a further implementation of GenAI, you should ask yourself the question: What do we expect? Efficiency? Control? Less risk? Or even a guarantee of success? In any case, a fantasy of control could prevent us from really rethinking communication. This would mean that we would only be using AI to reinforce what we are already doing, just doing it faster and more efficiently – if that is not already too euphoric. But how should we use GenAI to really make communication more creative and different?

This is one of the new management tasks in the GenAI era.
The fear of no longer being the master/woman of the process will only be reduced through practical application, when it becomes clear that AI serves as a tool that is controlled and monitored by human communicators to ensure the desired message is delivered.

Data protection concerns in the use of Generative AI

The use of AI in companies often raises questions about data protection and data security. AI systems process large amounts of data, often including sensitive information. This can raise concerns about compliance with data protection laws and data security. To address these challenges, it is essential to implement clear policies and measures to protect personal data.

A first step is to ensure that data processing by the AI systems complies with the applicable data protection regulations. This includes obtaining the necessary consent, minimizing data collection to the minimum

The use of artificial intelligence (AI) in companies offers numerous advantages, but also entails considerable risks for data protection. When processing personal data in particular, companies must ensure that the General Data Protection Regulation (GDPR) and other relevant data protection laws are strictly adhered to. The GDPR sets out clear rules on how data may be processed and requires companies to take appropriate technical and organizational measures to ensure the protection of personal data.

A central instrument for assessing data protection risks when using AI is the data protection impact assessment (DPIA). It enables companies to identify and evaluate potential sources of risk and define appropriate risk reduction measures. By carrying out a DPIA, companies can ensure that their AI systems are used in compliance with data protection regulations and that the rights of data subjects are protected.

In addition, companies should pay attention to principles such as "privacy by design" and "privacy by default" when using AI. This means that data protection aspects are already taken into account during the development of AI systems and data protection-friendly default settings are implemented by default. Regular audits and employee training in dealing with AI and data protection can also help to minimize risks and ensure compliance with data protection regulations.

It is also important to note that with the entry into force of the AI Regulation (KI-VO) on August 1, 2024 and the subsequent transition periods, further regulations must be observed when using AI. The first rules of the AI Regulation will apply from 2 February 2025, so companies should familiarize themselves with the new requirements at an early stage and adapt their AI systems accordingly to ensure compliance.

Overall, the data protection-compliant use of AI in companies requires a high degree of care and responsibility. By implementing appropriate measures and continuously reviewing data protection practices, companies can reap the benefits of AI without jeopardizing the privacy of the data subjects.

Resistance against all kinds of upcoming change

Resistance to change is a common phenomenon in companies, especially when established processes are called into question. Employees often experience uncertainty or fear of the unknown, which can lead to rejection, even if the changes could bring long-term benefits.

An effective approach to countering this resistance is to try things out and learn together. By actively involving teams in the change process, they can try out new ways of working and provide direct feedback. This participatory approach promotes understanding of the need for change and reduces anxiety. It also enables employees to contribute their experiences and perspectives, which increases acceptance.

Active participation in shaping change plays a decisive role here. When employees are given the opportunity to help shape change, they feel valued and taken seriously. This strengthens their commitment and willingness to adopt new processes. Managers should therefore create transparency, promote open communication and encourage their teams to get actively involved.

An open culture of error is essential for dealing with change in a positive way. In such a culture, mistakes are not seen as failures, but as learning opportunities. This encourages employees to try out new things without fear of negative consequences. Managers should act as role models by admitting their own mistakes and encouraging a constructive approach to them.

By combining these approaches – joint experimentation, active participation and an open error culture – the widespread aversion to change in established processes can be overcome. This leads to a more flexible and adaptable organization that is ready to face the challenges of the future.

PR
MARKET
& MARKETING

 would now like to recommend the first steps for the integration of AI if you are about to introduce GenAI into your communications department – whether PR or marketing.

This requires a systematic analysis of the potential that this offers along a timeline, early involvement of employees, clear guidelines for trial and series production and a phase of joint learning.

Below are the seven most important recommendations for action.

nalysis of demand

- Identify areas where AI offers the most added value
- Plan the subsequent human-machine workflow from the outset
- Prioritize resources and create an initial roadmap

This first step is to identify areas in PR & marketing where AI can offer the greatest added value. This could include the automation of repetitive tasks, the analysis of large amounts of data or the personalization of content for the respective stakeholders. A thorough needs analysis will help to understand the specific needs of the department and select appropriate AI solutions.

Prioritize AI applications that large parts of the team perceive as added value or relief.

It is also important to plan the future human-machine workflow from the outset. This includes defining roles and responsibilities and determining how humans and machines can work together effectively. Finally, by prioritizing resources and creating an initial roadmap, you ensure that the implementation is structured and targeted

Use the make-or-buy principle to differentiate between off-the-shelf solutions and those that still need to be developed or customized. And draw up a target picture from the outset of how you want to integrate the individual applications into an overall solution.

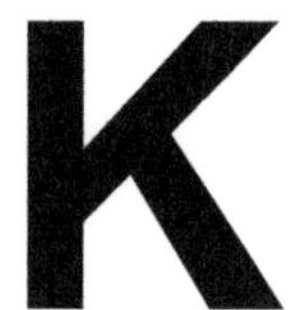ick-off with the team

- Familiarize the communications team with AI basics
- Sharing an initial vision for the future with everyone
- Creating space for the team's concerns and questions
- jointly identify potential applications

A successful start requires the communications team to be familiarized with the basics of AI. This can be done through training, workshops or information events or with "snackable content" at lunchtime (formats such as "Knowledge2Go" or "AI Change Café" have been created for this purpose, depending on whether the aim is to communicate facts or to set out on a journey of change). In any case, sharing a common vision for the future and involving the entire team in the process promotes commitment and acceptance.

It is essential to create space for the team's concerns and questions. Open discussions make it possible to reduce fears and jointly identify potential applications. This collaborative approach ensures that all members feel heard and can actively contribute to the success of the integration.

 **ramework for the use of GenAI**

- Create clear guidelines for data protection and data security
- Develop awareness of ethically correct use
- Establish clarity about the process for approving new AI tools and their central control

Creating clear guidelines for data protection and data security is essential. This not only protects sensitive information, but also creates trust among all parties involved. Developing an awareness of the ethically correct use of AI helps to minimize potential risks and act responsibly. The buy-in of employee representatives will also depend on this framework, as GenAI is to a large extent about the processing of data. It must be made clear that employee data is not processed by the language model at any time and, if applicable, that the language model itself is a local copy and is not trained outside the company with its data.

There should be clarity about the process for approving new AI tools and managing them centrally. This ensures that all technologies used comply with the defined standards and can be effectively integrated into existing systems. Communicators often need solutions that could also be of interest to other business areas. A good GenAI framework creates clarity and synergies and thus accelerates implementation.

Transparency at all times

- Mark content created by GenAI
- Transparency to maintain the trust of all stakeholders

Automated content should be clearly labeled. This transparency maintains the trust of all stakeholders and prevents misunderstandings. Open communication about the use of AI in content creation strengthens credibility and promotes a positive perception.

There is currently no general legal obligation in Europe to label AI-generated content as such. However, in certain cases, labeling may be necessary to avoid misleading information, especially when AI content is mixed with human works, giving the impression that it is of human origin.

The legal situation will change with the entry into force of the EU AI Act. The AI Act, the world's first comprehensive legal framework for artificial intelligence, was adopted by the European Parliament on May 21, 2024 and gradually came into force as of February 2025.

One of the provisions of the AI Act stipulates that so-called "deepfakes" – i.e. AI-generated image, sound or video content that resembles real people, circumstances or events and could be considered authentic – must be clearly labeled as such for recipients (for example by adding phrases such as "created with AI support" or "powered by AI"). This labeling requirement is intended to ensure transparency and strengthen public trust in digital content.

It is important to note that this labeling requirement does not apply to all AI-generated content, but specifically to content that has the potential to mislead users. Companies and individuals using AI technologies should therefore familiarize themselves with the upcoming regulations and prepare appropriate measures to label their content in order to comply with future legal requirements.

In addition to the legal requirements, it is recommended that AI-generated content is labeled voluntarily for reasons of transparency and ethics. This can help to strengthen the trust of target groups and avoid misunderstandings. Perhaps in future, some social media posts will include a note such as "created by AI, edited by Susanne").

Pilot projects

- Start with pilot projects in defined areas
- Gather experience and make adjustments
- only then implementation on a broader level

Starting with pilot projects in defined areas makes it possible to gather initial experience and make any necessary adjustments. This controlled introduction helps to identify potential challenges at an early stage and develop solutions. Once the pilot projects have been successfully completed, implementation can take place on a broader scale.

A Proof of Concept (PoC) is a valuable method to test and validate the introduction of Generative Artificial Intelligence (GenAI) in a company. Here are the main benefits of such an approach:
A Proof of Concept (PoC) is a valuable method for testing and validating the introduction of Generative Artificial Intelligence (GenAI) in a company.

1. risk minimization
- **Feasibility testing:** A PoC makes it possible to test the technical and practical feasibility of a GenAI solution before large-scale implementation.
- **Identification of weak points:** Potential challenges and risks can be identified and addressed at an early stage before major investments are due.

- **Calculated test run:** Companies can carry out realistic tests without jeopardizing high investments or the entire communication process.

2. cost control

- **Reduction of unnecessary expenditure:** A clearly defined PoC helps to avoid unnecessary expenditure on unsuitable tools or technologies.
- **Focused use of resources:** Companies can invest limited resources in promising approaches in a more targeted manner.

3. gaining knowledge

- **Realistic insights:** A PoC provides concrete data on how well GenAI works in specific application areas, e.g. in content creation or data analysis.
- **Transparency:** Because a pilot project always has a beginning and an end and a limited use case, the advantages and disadvantages of the chosen solution(s) become apparent more quickly.
- **Iterative learning process:** Findings from a PoC can be used to adapt the strategy for implementation and scaling to the large use case.

4. internal acceptance

- **Practical relevance:** In a pilot project, gray theory quickly becomes concrete practice, which makes the new technology tangible and acceptable for many.
- **Convincing stakeholders:** A successful PoC demonstrates the added value of GenAI for corporate communication and is suitable for reducing internal reservations.

- **Team involvement:** Employees can be involved in the testing process, which builds trust and reduces resistance.

5. faster scaling

- **Well-founded decisions:** A PoC provides a reliable basis for decision-making in order to design the rollout of the technology in an efficient and targeted manner.
- **Optimized processes:** By testing on a small scale, processes and workflows can be adapted before they are applied across the entire company.
- **Administrative acceleration**: When the PoC is approved by IT, purchasing and the works council, as well as during the subsequent transfer to series production, everyone involved is generally in favor of faster processing because "nothing is set in stone".

6. measurability of success

- **Define and test KPIs:** The PoC helps to define and check clear success criteria (e.g. time savings, quality of results). Define targets and KPIs to measure target achievement at the start and ensure regular evaluations and derivations.
- **Evaluation of the results:** The results of the PoC provide a solid basis for evaluating the long-term impact of the technology on the company.

A proof of concept is therefore an indispensable tool for companies wishing to introduce GenAI. It combines strategic thinking with pragmatic testing and ensures that the introduction is fast, effective, cost-efficient and future-proof.

T trainings

- Ensure optimal use of AI tools
- Regular training to keep the team up to date
- Mix of training courses, tutorials, practical workshops

Regular training is essential to ensure the optimal use of AI tools. A mix of training courses, tutorials and practical workshops keeps the team up to date and promotes the effective use of the technologies. This not only strengthens employees' skills, but also increases the efficiency and quality of communication work.

As already described in the first chapter on areas of application, GenAI can be used very well to create multimedia training content. The "With GenAI via GenAI" approach is consistent and convincing.

F eedback mechanisms

- Implement feedback mechanisms
- Structured collection of observations in pilot projects
- Error culture in which mistakes are seen as opportunities

When testing and introducing new GenAI applications, well thought-out feedback mechanisms are crucial to systematically achieve progress. The process starts with establishing clear channels for collecting and analyzing feedback from pilot projects. These mechanisms should work on multiple levels and collect targeted data from different stakeholders.

The implementation of feedback mechanisms is crucial for the continuous improvement process. A structured collection of observations in the pilot projects provides valuable insights and makes it possible to continuously optimize the use of AI. A culture of error is important here, in which mistakes are seen as opportunities, which promotes innovation and a willingness to learn within the team.

1. structured feedback collection

- **Regular evaluation meetings:** Project teams should hold weekly or monthly meetings in which challenges and successes in dealing with GenAI solutions are openly discussed.
- **Digital feedback platforms:** A central digital tool, such as an internal dashboard, can be used to document problems, suggestions for improvement and innovative ideas. Users should be able to share their experiences in real time.
- **Questionnaires and surveys:** In order to collect standardized data, specific questions can be asked about the efficiency, user-friendliness and output quality of the GenAI tools.

2. error analysis as a learning process

- **Error logs**: Systematic logging of malfunctions or unsatisfactory results provides information about weak points in the technology or workflows. It is important that the input providers also see what happens with the error messages, otherwise frustration will arise.

- **Root cause analyses:** For more serious problems, teams should identify the causes in order to develop lasting solutions.
- **Develop best practices:** Successfully solved problems should be documented and established as standard solutions.

3. integrate feedback into the optimization process

- **Iterative improvements:** Feedback should be used in an iterative process to gradually adapt and refine AI models or workflows.
- **Prioritization of adjustments:** Feedback should be analyzed and prioritized in order to tackle the most urgent and easiest to implement improvements first.
- **Fast response times:** Thanks to short feedback cycles, challenges can be responded to more quickly before they have a lasting impact on the workflow.

4. promotion of an open error culture

- **Positive error communication:** Managers should emphasize that mistakes are not seen as failures, but as learning opportunities. In this way, you support both the GenAI project team and your "computer colleague" right from the start.
- **Workshops on error culture:** Training and team workshops can help to normalize the handling of errors and promote innovative solutions. Only if everyone sees this huge transformation as a journey, as a pioneering project, will the acceptance of mistakes increase.

- **Rewarding transparency:** Employees who openly report challenges and mistakes should be recognized for doing so in order to encourage others to do the same.

5. long-term innovation through feedback
- **Trend and needs analysis:** In the long term, a systematic collection of feedback can help not only to improve existing applications, but also to identify new fields of application for GenAI.
- **Collaborative learning:** By sharing their experiences and solutions, teams can create a shared knowledge base that extends beyond individual projects.
- **Feedback reviews:** Regular reviews of collected feedback and the resulting changes strengthen the culture of continuous improvement for other areas as well.

A well-structured feedback mechanism transforms pilot projects into learning loops that not only optimize the introduction of GenAI, but also promote innovation and team cohesion. In this way, the integration of AI in PR & marketing can be successfully designed because both technical and human aspects are taken into account

For friends of checklists, I have summarized the most important steps for you on the following pages. Simply tick what is relevant for you:

Section	Task	relevant	done
Analysis Planning	1. **carry out a needs analysis:** Identify areas where GenAI offers the greatest added value (e.g. content creation, media monitoring).		
	2. **define goals:** Define clear KPIs for the use of GenAI (e.g. time savings, quality improvement).		
	3. **determine budget:** plan resources for tools, training and implementation.		
	4. **market and tool analysis:** evaluate and compare available GenAI technologies.		
	5. **check the legal situation:** Consider data protection, copyright and possible obligations of GenAI labeling.		
	6. **plan human-machine workflow:** clarify roles/responsibilities between AI and team members		
	7. **involve stakeholders:** Involve management, data protection officers and relevant departments at an early stage.		

Section	Task	relevant	done
	8. **get support:** don't reinvent the wheel, but allow advice and action from outside to learn from positive and negative experiences		
	9. **kick-off with the team:** Present GenAI basics and share vision.		
Preparation / Teamwork	10. **train the team:** Offer workshops on the planned tools and their functions.		
	11. **gather concerns:** Create space for questions and concerns in order to reduce resistance.		
	12. **define pilot projects:** Define clear areas of application and test phases.		
	13. **develop a communication strategy:** Plan internal and external communication for the introduction of GenAI.		
	14. **establish feedback mechanisms:** set up a structured collection of feedback.		
	15. **install tools:** Set up the selected GenAI tools technically and manage access.		

Section	Task	relevant	done
Implementation / testing	16. **check the data basis:** Ensure that AI models work with current, relevant data.		
	17. **carry out content test:** Have initial content created by GenAI and evaluate results.		
	18. **test automation:** automate processes such as social media planning or sentiment analysis.		
	19. **implement pilot projects:** Start test run within a clearly defined framework.		
	20. **document results:** Collect feedback and key performance indicators from the pilot projects.		
	21. **promote a culture of error:** Address problems openly and use them as learning opportunities.		
	22 **Iterative improvements:** Using feedback to optimize tools and processes.		

Section	Task	relevant	done
Optimization / Scaling	23 **Review ethical standards:** Ensure GenAI deployments are in line with company values.		
	24 **Strengthen collaboration:** Encourage team members to use GenAI as a tool for creative and strategic tasks.		
	25 **Evaluate KPIs:** Check progress and target achievement based on the defined KPIs.		
	26. **adapt processes:** Optimize workflows and guidelines based on the test results.		
	27. **prepare for scaling:** Expand successful pilot projects to other areas or campaigns.		
	28. **ensure content labeling:** Clearly mark GenAI-generated content as such.		

Section	Task	relevant	done
Transparency / communication	29. **communicate successes:** Internal and external communication about the benefits and results of using GenAI.		
	30. **regular reviews:** Ongoing review of the GenAI strategy and its impact.		
	31. **obtain stakeholder feedback:** consider the opinions of customers, partners and other stakeholders.		
	32. **regular training:** Continuously train the team on new functions and developments.		
	33. **follow technological developments:** Monitor and evaluate new GenAI tools and trends.		

Section	Task	relevant	done
Long-term further development	34. **expand fields of application:** check potential in areas such as customer support or market analysis.		
	35. **cooperation with partners:** promote exchange with external experts or agencies.		
	36 **Develop a long-term strategy:** Establish GenAI as an integral part of the communication strategy.		
	37. **share success stories:** Documenting and passing on best practices and lessons learned.		

Generative artificial intelligence requires us all to learn many new things. That's why I want to conclude this short guide with some basic insights that I have gained in my first two years with GenAI. Starting with the question of whether communication will actually be fully automated at some point, through the sense and nonsense of prompt seminars, to a technology that opens up further valuable context for GenAI in addition to the messages: the vectorized RAG file storage.

The fundamental considerations also include the question of which type of content will win out in the ongoing battle for attention in the future. Then I want to share a paradox with you that I came across: GenAI as a self-referencing system

And at the end I explain transparently how GenAI supported me in writing this book.

Full automation of communication as a vision?

Regardless of whether we, as a society based on the division of labor and a market economy, would even want to see full automation in certain sectors of the economy, this question is initially a technical one. Has the total automation of processes without human intervention become conceivable in the communications industry, for example, with GenAI?

Full automation can only encompass what can be automated at all. If we assume that human skills of commissioning, assessing and confirming will continue to be needed in the future – either because we want this as a society so that our economic system works, or because these skills cannot be replaced by algorithms so quickly – then only hybrid automation can be the goal.

In order to integrate AI solutions into the daily practice of a communications department in such a hybrid way, it can be advantageous to bundle them in an application that takes care of the planning, production, distribution and evaluation of communication as a whole. GenAI fits seamlessly into the processes when workflows between humans and algorithms are created in the central application so that they play into each other's hands. Various AI bots with different skills and authorizations join the process one day without being asked and offer their help. This is the future of communication!

On the sense and nonsense of prompt seminars

By the mid-twenties, most communicators had already attended one or more prompt seminars, probably violated countless requirements from their IT departments and, after trying out dozens of unique AI tools, wished there wasn't such a rocky road between deployment maturity and series production.

In the meantime, the business model of prompt seminars will soon be obsolete again, as technology is advancing to such an extent that AI prompts could become increasingly superfluous. One thing to bear in mind is that, after all, the machine has evolved from humans in the level of abstraction from machine code of zeros and ones to the first programming languages such as assembler to higher programming languages such as Fortrun or C++ to understanding spoken key terms and, today, finally to understanding natural language. The evolution from machine-oriented programming to natural language shows how much technology aims to adapt to humans and abstract away complexity.

We are actually on the verge of interaction with machines becoming almost completely "human". It feels like we have reached 99 percent abstraction level. The last percent is probably the most difficult because it involves not only technological but also cognitive challenges – such as understanding context, emotions, ambiguity or even non-verbal communication. Many of the challenges, such as understanding context and finer nuances in communication, are being tackled rapidly. There has been impressive progress in understanding natural language, images and even emotional undertones.

At a certain point, it's less about whether the technology is perfect and more about how natural it feels for the user. When people hardly notice the difference between an AI interaction and a human one – or an AI content and a human-made content – then it will almost feel like reaching the "last percent". Because then you hardly have to spend any time on technical details and can concentrate fully on the content. It can be assumed that for many use cases, this "last percent", which turns a human-machine interface into what feels like a "human-human interface", will be reached before 2030. A lot depends on how well AI is able to simulate real human intuition and deep understanding.

So what's the point of prompt seminars? The idea of creating humanoid robots to make computers seem more human and then telling users to look up the best way to talk to these robots or AI assistants in a dictionary or user manual sounds absurd. After all, the vision is that you speak to them as naturally as you do to other people, without having to think about specific formulations. At best, people could use prompt seminars to practise logical, clear and structured thinking and speaking again. This is something we humans have partially lost in a hectic age of multitasking and constant distractions. We will see AI becoming more and more of a creative partner instead of just a tool that executes strict commands.

Context with vectorized files in the RAG store

The integration of GenAI into communication processes requires that the AI has access to relevant knowledge in order to provide meaningful and contextualized answers. I described at the beginning how you can store the essence of your communication in a digital one-voice message library. An effective way to provide further context is to use vectorized files in RAG storage. In this section, I highlight the basics, benefits and implementation steps of this technology.

What is a RAG storage facility?

Retrieval augmented generation refers to the generation of content with information that is optimized for fast retrieval. Specifically:

- **Retrieval:** A system searches external knowledge sources to find relevant information.
- **Generation (generation):** A language model uses the retrieved information to create a response or text.

Why vectorized files?

A RAG store stores vectorized data. Vectors describe the location of content in the multidimensional space of meaning. To obtain vectors for the uploaded files, an AI model is used to analyze them semantically. The numerical representation of texts, images or other content in vectors enables fast and context-accurate retrieval.

This allows similar content to be found next to each other. This speeds up searches and makes content comparable. And suitable answers to questions can be found more quickly. The decisive factor in vectorization is that it does not depend on specific formulations, but purely on the meaning. Even the language of the context material is irrelevant.

Traditional database-based approaches work with exact matches. To do this, however, you have to use the exact keywords that are stored in the database query. When formulating the search query, you therefore had to somehow anticipate the answer so that you used the correct query (search term). Vectorized files, on the other hand, enable a broad semantic search, which takes into account the meaning of a request, even if the wording is different.

One example:

- **Inquiry**: "How do I optimize my workflow?"
- **Hits**: Semantically, sections such as "Efficient time management" or "Productivity tips" could also fit.

Advantages of the RAG storage facility

1. **Contextual accuracy:** AI can retrieve relevant information from large knowledge bases. The more context, the better the results.

2. **Scalability:** Even with millions of documents, the search remains performant, i.e. it does not take long.

3. **Adaptability:** The memory can be regularly updated with new content. This is in stark contrast to the fine-tuning of language models. Subsequent changes are almost impossible, as the next section shows.

4. **Semantic depth:** Thanks to vectorization, the system recognizes contexts of meaning that go beyond simple keywords.

Advantage of a RAG store compared to fine-tuning a language model

A RAG store can be easily and regularly updated with new content. Vectorizing new data and adding it to the vector index is a comparatively fast and scalable process. As soon as new data is introduced, it is directly available to the AI for queries to . This makes RAG particularly flexible, as information can be added or removed dynamically without having to retrain the entire system.

Fine-tuning a language model, on the other hand, is a complex and resource-intensive process. The model is trained with additional data in order to acquire specific knowledge or adapt to a particular use case. Fine-tuning has the following restrictions:

- **Time required:** Fine-tuning often takes several hours or even days, depending on the model size and data set.
- **Costs:** Powerful hardware and considerable computing resources are required.
- **Static nature:** Once a model has been fine-tuned, it is "fixed". To add new content, the model would have to be trained again, which can overwrite the previous adjustments or make them unstable.
- **Memory requirements:** Fine-tuning leads to a new model version that requires additional memory.

RAG technology is therefore more flexible and much easier to maintain, as it can be updated continuously and without lengthy retraining. Fine-tuning, on the other hand, is less dynamic for dealing with frequently changing content that is deliberately not to be deeply embedded in the language model.

Steps for implementing a RAG storage system

1. **Data preparation:**

   - In addition to messages, collect relevant texts, documents, board resumes, product data sheets, FAQs, style guides, corporate spelling, other sources of knowledge.
   - Clean and standardize the data before using it in the RAG store (removal of duplicates, correction of formatting errors).
   - For each document that you upload, define a responsible person in the team who should confirm that the document is up-to-date at certain intervals (preferably workflow-supported).

2. **Vectorization of the content:**

   - Use pre-trained models such as BERT, OpenAI's embeddings or Sentence Transformers to transform the texts into numerical vectors.
   - Each text is saved as a vector that represents its semantic content.

3. **Storage in the vector index:**

   - Use specialized databases such as Pinecone, Weaviate, Milvus or FAISS. These are optimized to search vectorized data quickly and efficiently.

4. **Retrieval mechanism:**

   - Integrate a retrieval process that identifies the nearest neighbors in the vector space (Nearest Neighbor Search) based on the user's query.

5. **Generation of answers:**

- Pass retrieved information to a generative model (e.g. GPT). The AI uses the content found to generate a coherent and well-founded answer.

Important experiences:

- **Quality of the data:** Only high-quality content delivers precise results. Invest time in data procurement and consolidation.
- **Fine-tuning:** If necessary, adapt the generative model to your specific domain. However, you should only do this with static (e.g. historical) information that will not change in a few years.
- **Validation and data maintenance:** Regularly check the relevance and up-to-dateness of the retrieved content.
- **Security:** Anonymize sensitive or personal data or exclude it from RAG storage to comply with data protection regulations.

A RAG repository with vectorized files is a powerful tool to make artificial intelligence more effective in communication. By combining semantic search and generative text processing, organizations can deliver context-rich and precise answers that meet the requirements of modern communication systems. With the right preparation and implementation, you can take the next step in AI-powered communication.

The battle for attention reaches new heights with GenAI

In social media such as X or LinkedIn, on YouTube or TikTok, we are already experiencing a vast amount of texts, photos, videos and audio tracks that are not made by people, but which many people take at face value

This is a social problem when people – including those from abroad – are manipulated and unsettled, when elections and entire political systems are destabilized as a result. Or when white-collar criminals prepare their deeds with deceptively genuine deepfakes. At the end of the day, the credibility of the media – and ultimately of all senders – is at risk

And all this while the battle for media attention continues to intensify. Some will try deep fakes to drive up follower, click and like statistics, others will use authenticity and originality to stand out from the possible AI monotony (which arises especially when the technology is not used properly).

AI by no means relieves communicators of their inherent task of discovering special angles for stories they have to tell about their companies.

Fake, nonsense, artifacts awaken a need for authenticity, quality journalism with gatekeepers and for quality communication work. Because trust is the most important currency of our time. Who can I still trust as a citizen, as a voter, as a consumer? This is our common lever as communicators. It should encourage our profession, whether journalists or press spokespersons.

Self-referencing system: When GenAI content trains GenAI

And finally, I would like to point out a more theoretical problem that I encountered in my analysis. This is not something that users have to deal with, but AI scientists do.

Until now, language models have been trained with the help of texts written by humans, to a large extent not only from libraries and their masterpieces, but also with countless sources from the internet. This explains the broad world knowledge that resonates with the current LLMs. This also explains some of the spelling and grammatical errors in the first-generation AI texts – all too human, you could say. But it also explains why some AI-generated content reflects our very own human way of putting things into words.

But what if more GenAI texts than human texts are used as training material from day X? Will the approximation of algorithms to humans then end and will Generative Artificial Intelligence become a self-referencing system? This must be prevented.

Help with writing: How GenAI supported me in this book

By 2016, the first computer would win a Pulitzer Prize, predicted Kris Hammond from US technology company **Narrative Science** five years earlier. 90 percent of journalism would be written by machines by 2030. He earned a weary smile...

January 2024: When 33-year-old Japanese author **Rie Kudan** receives the prestigious Akutagawa Prize in Tokyo (comparable to the Pulitzer Prize in the USA), she makes a confession in her acceptance speech. In the writing process, she used programs such as ChatGPT. "I probably took around five percent of the book verbatim from AI-generated sentences

The American artist **Jason Allen** already won an art prize in Colorado in 2022, even though he had submitted a picture created by the AI image generator Midjourney

Canadian author **Stephen Marche** even had 95 percent of his mystery novel "Death of An Author" written by AI.

For the sake of good order, I won't make a secret of it, even if you probably wouldn't have noticed because of the low dose: **I also asked for help.**

First, I wrote down my own credo on the topic, my core messages so to speak. Then I had GenAI formulate a paragraph from each message and quickly realized where my briefing was clear enough and where I needed to intervene. Only when all the paragraphs were in line with my thinking and writing did I ask GenAI again to write three to four from each paragraph. Again, there were many good ideas, and some that I immediately discarded.

In the end, I would say: 15 percent GenAI, 85 percent me. And I stand behind every word with my name because I have tweaked, improved, rearranged and reformulated it. I was guided by my experience and convictions, not the algorithms.

Finally, I asked myself the question: What conclusion would GenAI itself draw if it were simply asked to do so with the following prompt?

PROMPT: *End the book on AI in corporate communications with a positive thought, derived from "Pandora's Box".*

RESULT:

> Artificial intelligence in corporate communications may seem like a modern-day Pandora's box – full of uncertainties, challenges and ethical questions. But just like in the original mythology, one thing remains amidst all this complexity: hope.
>
> The hope that AI not only accelerates processes, but also opens new doors for authentic dialog and creative solutions. The hope that technology will not replace people, but strengthen them – by creating space for what makes us unique: empathy, innovation and the ability to build relationships.

When companies use AI responsibly, with a clear focus on transparency and humanity, Pandora's box becomes a treasure chest full of potential. It is up to us to unleash this potential and carry it into a future in which technology and people work hand in hand – for communication that connects.

There is nothing to add to this. I wish you every success with GenAI!

Yours
Richard Tigges

All illustrations in this book were created with GenAI.

G lossary

A

Agenda surfing: the strategic use of current trends and topics to place your own messages in relevant contexts and maximize attention

AIAD: Artificial Intelligence Assisted Design with the use of AI to support design processes

Altastic: an innovative German start-up for media intelligence that offers media monitoring and analysis based on AI

Asset: in communication, a valuable multimedia content, such as texts, images, videos or data, which are used strategically

Asset management: the management and optimization of assets for efficient use for PR & marketing, including the storage of usage rights

Audiate: an application from Techsmith® that converts audio and video content into text to facilitate editing

Avatar: a digital, personalized representation of a person or brand used in virtual or AI-driven environments

B

BERT: an AI model from Google that semantically texts from natural language

Message library: a collection of pre-formulated strategic core messages for communication

C

Change Café: a space (physical or digital) where teams can meet informally to discuss and shape changes

Chatbot: an AI-supported virtual assistant that answers text or voice queries from users

Content: Content such as texts, images, videos or interactive media that are to be published

Data protection: the protection of personal data from unauthorized access or misuse

Data security: measures and technologies aimed at protecting data from loss, theft or manipulation

Deepfake: an AI-generated manipulation of videos or images to make people look deceptively real

E

Elevenlabs: an online platform that offers speech synthesis, voice cloning and video dubbing for various language versions

EU AI Act: a legislative framework of the European Union for the regulation of artificial intelligence with a focus on security, transparency and ethics

F

FAISS: an open source tool from Facebook for fast similarity searches in large data sets

Fine-tuning: the process of adapting a pre-trained AI model to specific requirements or domains (versus RAG)

Flick: an online platform for the creation, optimization and distribution of social media content

Framework: the legal, ethical, technical and organizational framework for the implementation and operation (here: of GenAI applications), see also Governance

G

Generative Artificial Intelligence, or GenAI for short: AI systems that can generate new content such as text, images or music

Generative Engine Optimization (GEO): Strategies for optimizing content so that it is better found by AI assistants

Governance: the legal and de facto regulatory framework for managing and monitoring an organization; here: Guidelines and processes that ensure the responsible use of AI.

GPT or Generative Pre-trained Transformer: An AI model that generates texts by training and processing large amounts of text data in advance

H

HeyGen: Californian start-up with software for generating GenAI video content and avatars

Hyper-personalization: the use of AI to create highly personalized content or experiences based on data analysis

J

JasperAI: AI-supported writing tool that generates texts for various use cases

K

KPI (Key Performance Indicator): Key figure for the success or progress of strategies and measures

L

LLM (Large Language Model): a language model such as GPT, Llama

M

Media monitoring: the monitoring of media channels to identify relevant mentions, trends or topics

Media analysis: the systematic evaluation of media content in order to gain insights into reach, impact or sentiment.

Message tracking: the (worldwide) tracking of communication messages with the help of semantic vectorization

Milvus: an open source platform for managing and searching vectorized data

N

Nearest Neighbor Search: an algorithm that identifies the most similar data points in a vectorized data set

O

One-voice policy: Definition of core statements and language rules for consistent use by all representatives of a company as part of strategic communication

OpenAI's embeddings: an AI model from OpenAI that semantically vectorizes text from natural language

Outside-in impulses: external perspectives or suggestions for internal decision-making

P

Performance: the effectiveness or efficiency of a campaign, usually measured by KPIs such as reach, engagement, share of positive voice compared to the competition

Pinecone: a platform for storing and managing vectorized data, optimized for AI applications

PoC (proof of concept): a prototype or test that demonstrates the feasibility of a concept

Prompt library: a collection of ready-made input instructions (prompts) for AI systems

R

RAG or Retrieval Augmented Generation: a method in which AI models retrieve additional information using semantic vectors to generate more precise answers (versus fine-tuning)

S

Self-referencing system: a system that trains on the basis of its own data and learns nothing more in the process

Sentence Transformers: an AI model for converting texts into vectors for semantic similarity calculations

Sentiment: the emotional evaluation of texts as positive, neutral or negative

Sharing economy: business models based on the shared use of resources or services

Snackable content: short, easy-to-consume content that is specially optimized for digital platforms

Synthesia London start-up with software for generating GenAI video content and avatars

V

Vectorization: Conversion of texts into numerical vectors in order to locate them in the meaning space and thus sort them next to related texts

Voice cloning: the AI-supported replication of voices, often for personalized audio productions

Full automation: the state in which a process runs completely without human intervention

W

Weaviate: an AI-driven vector database that enables semantic search and knowledge management

Knowledge2Go: quickly accessible, compact knowledge formats, often in the form of podcasts or short videos

Workflow: a defined sequence of tasks and processes, often optimized through automation and documented in a verifiable manner

Y

YessPress® ComTool: a specialized software solution for content planning, production and distribution in PR & Marketing using the power of GenAI

A bbreviations

AI (Artificial Intelligence)

AIAD (Artificial Intelligence Assisted Design)

CEO (Chief Executive Officer)

dpa (German Press Agency)

EU AI Act (European Union Artificial Intelligence Act)

FAISS (Facebook AI Similarity Search)

GenAI (Generative Artificial Intelligence)

GEO (Generative Engine Optimization)

GPT (Generative Pre-trained Transformer)

IT (Information Technology)

KPI (Key Performance Indicator)

PoC (Proof of Concept)

PR (Public Relations)

Q&A (Questions and Answers)

RAG (Retrieval-Augmented Generation)

SEO (Search Engine Optimization)

UX/UI (User Experience/User Interface)